THIS BOOK WILL MAKE YOU SH!T YOURSELF

JAMES PROUD

summersdale

THIS BOOK WILL MAKE YOU SH!T YOURSELF

An Hachette UK Company
www.hachette.co.uk

Summersdale Publishers Ltd
Part of Octopus Publishing Group Limited
Carmelite House
50 Victoria Embankment
LONDON
EC4Y 0DZ
UK

www.summersdale.com

Printed and bound in China

ISBN: 978-1-78783-257-2

Substantial discounts on bulk quantities of Summersdale books are available to corporations, professional associations and other organizations. For details contact general enquiries: telephone: +44 (0) 1243 771107 or email: enquiries@summersdale.com.

IMPORTANT NOTE

The conspiracy theories contained in this book are just that: theories. The author and the publishers make no claim that any of these theories have any basis in fact. They are merely theories that have at some point been expressed in the public domain. Such theories are reproduced herein for entertainment purposes only and are not intended to be taken literally.

INTRODUCTION

Why do people like scary stories? The shudder in the chest? The sinking stomach? The racing heart rate and the tingle in the limbs? That feeling of being genuinely under threat?

This book contains a selection of the world's scariest, creepiest and most unnerving stories, legends and facts. From tales of extra-terrestrial encounters and ghostly happenings to true crime and unsettling conspiracies, it will send a shiver down your spine, and, well... you've read the title.

Many of the entries originate from a fear of the unknown: unidentified flying objects, unfathomable terror attacks, things that go bump in the night, the fear that secretive global elites are pulling our strings.

Whether the following stories are fact or fiction, reality or fantasy, is for you to decide. Are some things just too far-fetched to be a work of the imagination? After all, we all know that the world is scary place, but for you, it's about to get even scarier.

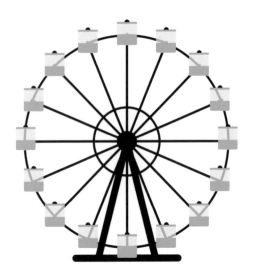

SCAREGROUND

In 2011 a new water ride at Thorpe Park Resort in Surrey, UK, was moved after workers reported a feeling of being watched, cold sensations, objects moving of their own accord and visions of a headless monk. The park managers called in paranormal experts who scanned the land and discovered evidence that the ride's foundations had disturbed an ancient burial ground. The area, known as Monk's Walk, was built in the year 666AD and was used by monks from nearby Chertsey Abbey.

OFF WITH HER HEAD

In 1864 Major-General James Durham Dundas was on duty in the Tower of London when he noticed a hooded woman gliding toward a guard in the courtyard below. The woman had no face. The guard thrust his bayonet into the intruder, but the figure walked right through him, giving him such a shock that he fainted. Only the testimony of Dundas as eyewitness saved the man from punishment for sleeping on the job. The ghost is said to have been Anne Boleyn, Henry VIII's second wife, executed in 1536 on charges of high treason.

HOLY SH!T

Anne Boleyn is said to stalk many of her old "haunts", including Hever Castle and Hampton Court Palace.

Each year on the anniversary of her death, she is said to arrive at the place of her birth, Blickling Hall in Norfolk, in a carriage drawn by a headless horseman, carrying her own head in her lap.

ANCIENT ALIENS

Our fascination with UFOs has spanned many civilizations, including ancient ones. In Lombardy, Italy, 10,000-year-old rock drawings depict figures wearing what look suspiciously like space helmets; hieroglyphs in 3,000-year-old tombs at Abydos, Egypt, depict helicopters and planes among birds and flying insects; and Hopi cave drawings in the South-Western United States feature what Native Americans called "star people" – legendary beings that arrived from space. Surely this can't be one huge coincidence?

HOLY SH!T

"Ancient alien" theorists believe that extraterrestrials were responsible for the erection of Stonehenge, the giant stone figures of Easter Island and even the extinction of the dinosaurs. It may sound a bit out there, but the seminal book on the topic, Erich von Däniken's Chariots of the Gods, *has sold over seven million copies.*

SLENDER MAN

In 2009, pictures began circulating online of children who had reportedly gone missing. All the images had something in common: looming in the background was a tall, thin figure dressed in black, with freakishly long arms and its face always obscured. In one image, a girl appears to be holding hands with the unsettling figure, and rumours spread that these were the last known photographs of the missing children. In 2014, the internet bogeyman made a shocking entry into the real world when two young girls killed a friend in Wisconsin, USA, telling the police that they did it to protect themselves from Slender Man.

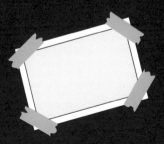

STIR-CRAZY IN STANFORD

In August 1971, 12 students were "arrested" by the Palo Alto Police Department, California, and transferred to cells at Stanford University, where they were strip-searched and each assigned a number. It was an experiment, with 24 students enlisted as "prisoners" or "guards" in a fake prison. The prisoners rebelled within 48 hours, barricading their cells. The guards responded with fire extinguishers and psychological abuse, forcing prisoners to strip naked, sleep on concrete and defecate in buckets. With the guards becoming increasingly sadistic and prisoners showing signs of "extreme stress", three of the students were released early and the experiment, set up to explore the effect of prisoner and guard roles on normal people, was abandoned after six days.

HOLY SH!T

Psychologists now cast doubt on the validity of the prison experiment, suggesting that the guards were encouraged to play up to the stereotype of a cruel prison guard, and that some were "acting" in order to help the experiment. It's also been alleged that the cruel treatment that the guards inflicted were suggested to them by the researchers in charge, undermining the idea that they became sadistic of their own accord.

THE BIG ONE IS OVERDUE

California is overdue for a massive earthquake. The past 100 years have been "unusually quiet" according to geologists. The last "Big One" hit San Francisco in 1906, killing 3,000 people and destroying 80 per cent of the city. In July 2019 the state experienced the biggest quakes for ten years, making some suspect that something is brewing underground. Los Angeles is thought to be the area most at risk. The city sits near the southern leg of the 800-mile San Andreas fault and hasn't experienced a big quake for more than 250 years.

DEADLY DIET PLAN

The Codex Alimentarius is a set of internationally agreed food standards, developed by the United Nations over decades. Not everyone thinks it's as healthy as it sounds and suspicious types have theorized that the codex is actually a secret plan for control of the global food supply by a shadowy elite who hide in plain sight. The cynics claim that the rules dictate that all food will eventually be irradiated and genetically manipulated, nutritional supplements and organic foods will be restricted and natural foodstuffs such as garlic will be reclassified as illegal drugs. The aim is to keep the population under control, in league with big drugs companies who will profit from providing "remedies" for malnutrition.

HOLY SH!T

Codex Alimentarius might sound obscurely ominous and like something out of The Da Vinci Code *– some even claim that the codex was written by Nazis after World War Two – but it just means "book of food" in Latin.*

VACUUM DECAY

According to a branch of physics called quantum field theory, the universe may have a fatal flaw. The Higgs field, a vital "quantum field" that gives all objects their mass, could be what scientists call a false vacuum. This means it is unstable and has huge amounts of potential energy. A high-energy random quantum event – which is not impossible – could create a "bubble" of energy in the Higgs field that would rampage across the universe at the speed of light, destroying everything in its path. Earth would be destroyed in a fraction of a second, and we wouldn't even see it coming.

SUB-ZERO SURPRISE

A rise in sea levels is not the only threat we face from climate change. The Arctic permafrost is thought to harbour bacteria and deadly viruses that have been there for thousands, even millions of years. These deadly microbes that are said to have infected early humans and Neanderthals could be resurrected as the ice melts. In fact, scientists have suggested that smallpox, anthrax, the Spanish flu and the bubonic plague are likely to be buried in Siberia.

HOLY SH!T

Climate change can also have unpredictable effects on other bacteria. It is believed that it was only a 1.5 degree change in temperature in the fourteenth century that caused a small microbe to develop into the Black Death, killing between 75 million and 200 million people.

THE MANDELA EFFECT

Darth Vader never said, "Luke, I am your father" and Humphrey Bogart never said, "Play it again, Sam" in *Casablanca*. These are examples of the Mandela Effect; when large numbers of people share a false memory. The term was coined by paranormal consultant Fiona Broome, who noticed that many people online were sure that they had seen news reports of Nelson Mandela's death in prison in the 1980s, when in reality he died in 2013. Some have speculated that the Mandela Effect is caused by glitches in alternate realities that exist independently of our own.

HOLY SH!T

- *Many people have posted online about a film called* Shazaam *that they watched in the 1990s, despite the film never existing.*

- *The queen in Disney's* Snow White *actually says "Magic mirror on the wall", not "Mirror, mirror on the wall".*

- *Forrest Gump actually said "Life was like a box of chocolates".*

OUIJA

Sally took advantage of her boyfriend David going away by hosting a party for her friends. At midnight after a couple of drinks, a Ouija board was produced. When the glass began to move, Sally asked:

"Are you dead?"

The glass traced out a reply, "Yes, Sally."

The group gasped. "How do you know my name?" asked Sally. "Who are you?!"

"I'm David. Answer the door."

Then they heard a knock.

THE SIMULATION HYPOTHESIS

In 2003 the philosopher Nick Bostrom penned an essay entitled "Are you living in a computer simulation?" in which he explored the possibility that humans may actually be computer code in a simulation run by a superior intelligence; possibly our own descendants. The thinking behind the hypothesis is that a superior intelligence with vast computing power runs many different simulations, for different uses, so it's more likely that we are part of one of those, and not the original *real* world, of which there is only one. Tech pioneer Elon Musk firmly believes in this theory, stating at a conference that "there's a billion to one chance we're living in base reality".

HOLY SH!T

Tech entrepreneurs take this theory so seriously that two Silicon Valley tech billionaires are reportedly funding secret research into the simulation; and how we can break out of it.

"Maybe our whole universe is a science experiment of some junior high-school student in another universe."
Ray Kurzweil,
Google Technology Director

DON'T WALK
TOWARD THE LIGHT

That hypnotic "bright light" reported by people who experience a near-death experience? It might be a trap. There's a school of thought, influenced by ancient gnostic spirituality, that the light is created by a malicious demiurge, an "interdimensional" being that enslaved humanity thousands of years ago. It employs false "angels" and dead relatives to tempt the dead back into its "matrix" (a term that predates the film of the same name), where it feeds on our souls in an endless cycle of birth and death.

LEFT BEHIND

The bag contained a pair of passports, wallets and other personal belongings. The find made the dive boat operator's blood run cold. Two days previously the Australian dive boat *Outer Edge* had carried an American couple 40 miles offshore to dive on the Great Barrier Reef. Only now did the crew realize that they had never returned to the boat. Months later, their diving gear was found washed up on a beach approximately 75 miles from where they were lost, including a dive slate on which the following message had been scrawled:

Monday Jan 26, 1998, 8am. To anyone [who] can help us. We have been abandoned on A[gin]court Reef by MV Outer Edge 25 Jan, 98, 3pm: Please help [come] to rescue us before we die. Help!!!

HOLY SH!T

Outer Edge actually returned to the same dive location the day after the missing couple, the Lonergans of Louisiana, had been abandoned. At this point nobody suspected anything, and when a diver found diving-belt weights at the bottom of the sea, likely dropped by the Lonergans, the crew regarded it as a "bonus". The bodies were never found.

ISN'T NATURE WONDERFUL

On average, 50 per cent of you reading this book have tiny creatures living on your eyelashes. At 0.5 mm long, demodex mites are almost invisible to the naked eye, and you would never know they are there, unless a particularly virulent infestation causes a skin condition. The eight-legged creatures burrow into eyelash hair follicles where they feed on sebum secreted by the skin. They can spend their entire lives on your face and can also be found hiding in the nose and ear canal.

GHOSTLY ATTACKERS

Doris Bither was a disturbed woman who sought the help of paranormal investigators at the University of California, including Dr Barry E. Taff. To their horror, Doris claimed that she had been repeatedly sexually assaulted by three ghostly entities, all invisible. Dr Taff and his team set up in Doris' house, where they were greeted by an odour of rotting flesh and cold spots. The team described unexplained lights appearing around Doris' bedroom, and a green mist in which a man's torso appeared. One team member fainted. Photographs of the incident show strange arcs of light, matching the reports of glowing orbs that Doris saw in her house.

HOLY SH!T

Soon after Doris moved into the house, she had a visit from an elderly Mexican lady who claimed to have once lived there. She warned: "You need to get out... There is something very evil here. This place is haunted and you need to get out."

THE PORT ARTHUR
MASSACRE CONSPIRACY

"It will take a massacre in Tasmania before we get gun reform," said Australian politician Barry Unsworth at a gun summit in 1987. In April 1996 Martin Bryant killed 35 people in a shooting at Port Arthur, and soon after the authorities passed strict gun control laws. Some believe that Bryant was a patsy for dark forces who committed the massacre to lay the ground for gun reform. They point to the fact that the suspect didn't go to trial (because he pleaded guilty) and the lack of motive, and they have questioned how an illiterate man with the mental age of an 11-year-old could have killed so many.

OLD HAG SYNDROME

You wake up in the middle of the night, unable to move. You can hear something, but can make no sound yourself. You sense a dark presence; something heavy is pressing on your chest. Then cold hands grab your arms… During sleep paralysis you are stuck in limbo between sleep and the waking world. Some believe that it's caused by visiting demons and witches; you just happened to catch them. One tip from doctors: don't sleep on your back, as it encourages the nightmares. Presumably, this is because it's harder for the demons to climb onto your chest when you're lying on your side.

HOLY SH!T

Tales of sleep paralysis take familiar forms in different cultures. The term "Old Hag syndrome" comes from Newfoundland, Canada. In China, the phenomenon is known as "ghost oppression", in Turkey, "the dark presser". The Japanese version is "Kanashibari", meaning to be tied up.

THE TROXLER EFFECT

Do try this at home: stare into a mirror in a dimly lit room for about ten minutes. According to an Italian study, you should start to notice facial deformations, visions of your parents' faces, mysterious strangers, old women, children, animals and "fantastical and monstrous beings". Scientists are not entirely sure why this happens, but they believe that it's linked to the Troxler effect, which describes the way your brain fades out visual features that you are not directly looking at.

THE HILL INCIDENT

On 19 September 1961, Barney and Betty Hill were driving through New Hampshire, USA, when a mysterious disc-shaped aircraft began silently hovering above them. They lost consciousness and awoke 36 miles away, losing 2 hours of memory. In 1964 they underwent hypnosis, and their accounts of that night were surprisingly consistent.

They both recounted how figures that were "somehow not human" forced them into a UFO, and they were separated and stripped naked. Barney remembered a tube being inserted into his rectum. Their abductors cut samples of Betty's hair, and a long needle was jabbed into her stomach – thought to be some form of pregnancy test – which caused agonizing pain. Then they were escorted back to their car.

HOLY SH!T

The Hill incident was America's first documented case of alien abduction. Betty's "pregnancy test" has been compared to modern keyhole surgery and amniocentesis, a test to detect genetic abnormalities in unborn babies that involves removing fluid from the uterus with a needle. In the early 1960s, the average American would have had no knowledge of either procedure.

FLOATING FEET AND GIANT SKELETONS

Dunster Castle in Somerset, which dates to the eleventh century, is one of Britain's most haunted buildings. Workers at the castle have reported being confronted by English Civil War soldiers and sightings of a disembodied human foot. In the nineteenth century a seven-foot-tall skeleton manacled at the wrists and ankles was discovered with other skeletons underneath the gatehouse in a cramped "oubliette" dungeon accessed only by a trapdoor. Nobody knows who he was, but he was likely locked up and left to starve with his unfortunate companions. Visitors report an eerie presence in the area, and dogs will refuse to go near.

THE RADIANT BOY

In September 1803 Reverend Henry Askew was staying in the oldest wing of Corby Castle in Cumbria, England, which dates to the fourteenth century. The clergyman was to visit for several days, but on the morning of 8 September he left in a hurry. He had awoken in the early hours to a glimmer in the centre of the room, which burst into flames and took on the shape of a boy. The flaming figure looked at Askew and then floated toward the fireplace, where it disappeared. A sighting of the "radiant boy" is said to bring great power; but also a tragic end. Askew was one of the lucky ones: he inherited a country estate after his brother died and lived to the age of 85.

HOLY SH!T

When the nineteenth-century British statesman Lord Castlereagh was a young man, he stayed in a large country house in a remote part of Ireland after getting lost. He too saw a radiant boy and heard the story of its curse. Castlereagh would rise to high office, but he became a hated figure, and in 1822, he cut his own throat.

WHO'S IN CONTROL?

The decisions you make can be correctly predicted before you are even conscious of making them. In 2008 scientists from Leipzig and Berlin, Germany, were able to use brain scanners to determine the choices made by test subjects up to 10 seconds before their conscious minds believed they had made the decisions. Other experiments since have had similar findings. If your brain is making decisions without you realizing, what does that mean for the concept of free will?

FINAL JOURNEY

Granger Taylor was a talented mechanic who spent his time restoring old vehicles. When he became interested in space travel, he built a large model of a flying saucer on the family farm. He also began to have dreams about communicating with aliens. In 1980, aged 32, Granger disappeared. He left a note:

I've gone away to walk aboard an alien spaceship, as recurring dreams assured a 42-month interstellar voyage to explore the vast universe, then return.

In a will Taylor left behind, he had changed "death" to "departure". But he did not return as promised, and he was never seen again.

YOUR NUMBER'S UP

In 2010 a Bulgarian mobile phone company retired the number 0888 888 888 after three people using it died in unusual circumstances in less than a decade. The first was the CEO of a telecoms company, who died of cancer aged 48. It's rumoured that he was poisoned with radiation by a rival. The next was a 31-year-old mafia boss, gunned down in the Netherlands, and finally a businessman who was assassinated outside a restaurant in Bulgaria's capital, Sofia.

HINTERKAIFECK MURDERS

In 1922 a series of incidents troubled a German farm, home to the Gruber family. Footsteps in the snow. Noises in the attic. A missing set of keys. Then the farm fell quiet. When neighbours investigated, they found the Grubers with their daughter and granddaughter in a barn, bludgeoned to death with a pickaxe. The bodies of young Josef Gruber and the family's housekeeper were in the farmhouse. There was no obvious motive, and the killer had apparently remained at the farm for days: the animals had been fed, smoke was seen and at least one local reported seeing a man. The killer was never found.

HOLY SH!T

More than 100 suspects were investigated for the killings at Hinterkaifeck, without success. The prime suspect was the Grubers' son-in-law, whose motive may have been revenge: his wife, Viktoria, had given birth to a son in his absence. The son, Josef, was rumoured to be a product of incest between Viktoria and her father, Andreas. However, the suspect had been declared missing-in-action during World War One and was likely dead himself.

THEBLINDMAIDEN.COM

According to various postings on internet message boards, supposedly originating in Spain, you can only visit the website www.theblindmaiden.com on the stroke of midnight, during a full moon, while you are alone. If you click accept you will be confronted with terror-stricken faces with black holes for eyes, fading to a live video that you realize is your own room. On your monitor you can see a female figure draped in black walking through the door behind you, but you daren't look around. As she moves closer, you see she is wearing a blood-soaked blindfold, before she tears your eyes out. Your face will be uploaded to the website for the next visitor.

CAMP AMERICA

It is said there are hundreds of concentration camps scattered around the United States, empty yet fully staffed, guarded by watchtowers and barbed wire, ready for an influx of enemies: American citizens. They are supposedly operated by FEMA, a sinister government agency that has the power to detain, and even kill, US citizens. FEMA, or the Federal Emergency Management Agency, is actually tasked with responding to disasters such as Hurricane Katrina, but many right-wing American "patriots" believe it has a darker purpose. When a "new world order" takes over, these patriots are sure they will be the first to be rounded up and detained in the ready-made death camps as enemies of the new global government.

HOLY SH!T

FEMA is actually involved with the setting up of camps, in line with US government policy, but only for humanitarian purposes. The notion that FEMA is building camps to detain enemies of the government has been around for decades, yet no such camps have ever been discovered.

REST IN PEACE?

Buncombe County, North Carolina, January 1885. A young man called Jenkins was declared dead after being sick with fever and was buried the next day. Two weeks later Jenkins was exhumed by relatives to be laid to rest in his family cemetery. The wooden coffin was opened to check the body's condition for the journey. What they saw horrified them. The body was lying face down, hair had been pulled from the head, and there were scratches on the *inside* of the box. At his burial, it had been remarked that Jenkin's body was as "limber as a live man". Now, at least, he was certainly dead.

COLD WAR CLOSE CALL

Stanislav Petrov was the commanding officer of a Soviet surveillance team in a bunker south of Moscow that operated an early-warning detection system for American nuclear missiles. On 26 September 1983, he received an alert that five nuclear missiles had been launched toward Russia. It was Petrov's duty to inform his superiors immediately, but he knew what that would mean: an all-out strike on US targets, or in other words, nuclear war. He froze. Why would the USA launch only five missiles, knowing the Soviets would retaliate? He delayed, and delayed. Twenty tense minutes later a false alarm was confirmed. Petrov's indecision had averted nuclear war.

THE ENFIELD MONSTER

On 25 April 1973, Henry McDaniel's children told him something was trying to get into his house in Enfield, Illinois. Upon investigating he heard scratching at the door. When he opened it, he expected a cat, but instead what he saw was a grey creature standing about four feet tall on three legs, with large red eyes. He slammed the door and fetched his pistol, returning to fire 4 times on the unidentified animal, but it hissed and fled, jumping 50 feet in a few leaps. The police found scratches in the door made by a six-clawed paw, not the usual four of domestic pets.

HOLY SH!T

The local police had received reports that day of an attack on a young boy who had his shoes shredded by a creature matching McDaniel's disturbing description. More than 30 years earlier, a similar creature was described in Mount Vernon, about an hour's drive from Enfield. It was blamed for local animal deaths and mutilations in the area, and was described as being capable of jumping huge distances.

REPOSSESSED

In 1928, 46-year-old Anna Ecklund of Iowa, USA, underwent her second exorcism. The first had occurred 16 years earlier, after she committed "unspeakable" sexual acts and developed an inability to enter churches. The rumours were that she had been cursed by her witch aunt and an abusive father. This relapse saw her committed to a convent, resisting those who restrained her with superhuman strength, spitting and vomiting food that had been blessed. She began speaking in tongues, and it's even claimed that the possession caused her to levitate. After finally shouting at her demons, including her father and aunt, to go to hell, she recovered.

CONNED-TRAILS

The white plumed "contrails" that planes leave behind in clear blue skies are not in fact condensed water vapour (clouds) but actually the stealth deployment of chemical weapons by shadowy forces. That is the claim of "chemtrail" conspiracies, which maintain that the trails are used to spread viruses, such as bird flu and Sars, in order to control the global population. Chemtrails are said to have originated from President Reagan's "Star Wars" anti-Soviet weapons technology in the 1980s.

HOLY SH!T

Chemtrails are blamed for numerous nefarious activities. Some think they are masking the effects of global warming, others that they are part of an American weather-control weapon, used to instigate events such as Hurricane Katrina.

GRAVE JUSTICE

In 1977 Chicago hospital worker Remy Chua started acting oddly; her behaviour culminated in her going into a trance-like state in which she began talking to her husband in a voice that was not her own. She claimed to be in the grip of a woman called Teresita Basa, a colleague who was the victim of a recent murder, as yet unsolved. She named Alan Showery as her killer and identified jewellery that he had stolen. Her husband contacted the police, who while sceptical, investigated the claims. Showery worked at the hospital, and he was in possession of the jewellery. He confessed and was convicted of the murder.

THE DIBBUK BOX

In 2004 a "dibbuk box" was put up for sale on eBay by a seller from Missouri. It had apparently brought a "tidal wave of bad luck" to the owner, causing their hair to fall out. The box's previous custodians were similarly cursed: a previous owner had suffered a stroke after receiving the box (she was able scrawl the message "HATE GIFT" afterward), and unpleasant odours, blurred vision and insect infestations were also reported. In Jewish folklore a "dibbuk", or "dybbuk", is the spirit of a dead person who enters the bodies of the living. The box's contents included locks of hair and some pennies (representing a date of birth) which would support the theory that it housed a restless spirit.

HOLY SH!T

When one of its owners set up a website dedicated to the box, he received emails from visitors to the site who complained of suffering headaches and nightmares after simply viewing photographs of the dibbuk box. Experts in Jewish mysticism have recommended that the box be buried in a full Jewish ceremony to put the spirit residing inside to rest.

CABIN 28

On 12 April 1981, 14-year-old Sheila Sharp entered cabin 28 on a resort in Keddie, California, and found the bodies of her mother, Sue Sharp, her brother John and his friend Dana. They had been bound, gagged and brutally murdered with hammer blows and stabbings. Their blood was all over the cabin. Sheila's sister Tina was missing, and bizarrely, the three younger children in the family were unharmed in another room. They seemed to have slept through the incident. Tina's remains were found three years later, 30 miles away. The crimes were never solved; it's been claimed that the two main suspects in the murder were protected by law enforcement due to their links to organized crime.

THE PHANTOM TIME HYPOTHESIS

According to the German historian Heribert Illig, the year 613 was immediately followed not by 614 but by 912, and great historical figures of the early Middle Ages, such as Holy Roman Emperor Charlemagne (742–814), simply never existed. The "phantom time hypothesis", first outlined by Illig in 1991, proposes that when the Julian calendar was replaced in 1582 by the Gregorian system after more than 1,600 years, it was out of sync with the solar year by 13 days, not the ten days for which it was adjusted. Illig eventually worked out that along with other "missing periods" in history, this accounted for 298 years that never existed. So it's actually the eighteenth century right now.

ELECTRICAL ARMAGEDDON

Without the Sun, there would be no life on Earth, but the star also poses a grave threat to civilization. It emits huge clouds of gas and radiation, called solar flares. Most are harmless, but a direct hit from a big solar flare could end life as we know it. The electromagnetic radiation would cause a huge solar storm that would knock out systems such as power grids, satellites, GPS, banking and the internet, causing at least $2 trillion in damage – equivalent to the entire GDP of the UK.

HOLY SH!T

In 1859 the largest solar storm on record occurred. The Carrington Event lit up the night sky like daylight and took down early telegraph systems, sparking fires. The effect on today's technology-reliant world could be far worse. In 1967 a solar flare set off an American early warning radar. The US military assumed a Soviet missile had been launched and almost launched a retaliatory strike before scientists worked out it was a false alarm.

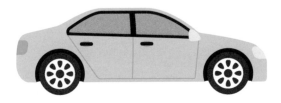

THE BURPHAM GHOST CRASH

On 11 December 2002, several motorists rang the police in Surrey, England, to report a car that veered off the A3 near Burpham. When officers arrived at the location, they could find no trace of an accident, until they came across a wrecked car hidden in undergrowth, out of sight of the road. It had clearly been there for quite some time. A decomposed body lay nearby. The car had crashed five months previously, but when the driver was reported missing, the police drew a blank. Had motorists that night seen a ghostly evocation of the original crash, leading police to the missing person?

DARK DISNEY DOLLS

"It's a Small World" is a water ride that has been a fixture of Disneyland parks around the world since the early 1970s. Hundreds of moving child dolls in traditional world costumes sway and sing along to the song that the ride is named after. That's probably creepy enough, but some say that dead staff members who worked on the ride liked it so much that their spirits haunt the tunnels. It's said that after hours the lights turn on and off, and the dolls perform for the ghosts, even though the power is off.

HOLY SH!T

A picture that went viral online purports to show the inside of the "It's a Small World" show in the midst of a passenger evacuation after the lights went out and the ride shut down. The dim image shows a small figure hanging from the ceiling.

CHARLIE, ARE YOU THERE?

In 2015 the #CharlieCharlieChallenge hashtag went viral on social media. Here's how to play: Balance one pencil across another on a sheet of paper to form a grid, with "yes" or "no" written in the squares. Then ask, "Charlie, are you there?" If the top pencil spins toward "yes", then you've summoned a Mexican demon, Charlie, who will answer further questions, but only until he gets bored; then he might seek a different kind of entertainment.

Players are advised to request politely an end to the visitation, or they risk allowing potentially malevolent forces to come and go as they please. In 2016 it was reported that 22 teenagers suffered a "mass demonic possession", screaming, hallucinating and foaming at the mouth, after playing the game at a school in the Chocó region of Colombia.

EXPERIMENTS IN THE REVIVAL OF ORGANISMS

In 1940 the Soviet authorities released a film in which two scientists, Sergei Brukhonenko and Boris Levinskovsky, drained all the blood from a dog, waited for several minutes, then attached a "heart-lung" machine which pumped the blood back into the animal. The dog's heart restarted, and apparently it went on to live a healthy canine life. They had brought it back from the dead.

In 2005, US scientists replicated the results, reanimating dogs that had been dead for several hours by replacing their blood with saline solution before pumping the blood back into their bodies. Such experiments provide hope to some that scientists will one day be able to put humans into suspended animation – a temporary state in which bodily functions are slowed or stopped completely.

HOLY SH!T

Soviet scientists carried out many cruel and unusual experiments. In the 1950s Vladimir Demikhov made headlines after transplanting the severed heads of dogs onto other canines, creating several two-headed creatures, one of which lived for several weeks. Demikhov's gruesome work made an important contribution to modern transplant medicine.

IT IS NOT AN AIRCRAFT

"It seems to me that he's playing some sort of game. He's flying over me at speeds I cannot identify."

Australian pilot Frederick Valentich was flying over the Bass Strait in October 1978 when he radioed air traffic control about a mysterious aircraft. There were no known planes in the vicinity.

"Can you describe the aircraft?"

"It's a long shape...

The thing is just orbiting on top of me – also, it's got a green light and sort of metallic like it's all shiny on the outside... It is hovering and it's not an aircraft."

There was no record of any further transmissions from the aircraft. Valentich was never heard from again.

THE VISITORS

On 24 April 1964, Sergeant Lonnie Zamora was following a suspect in the desert in New Mexico, USA, when he heard a loud roar and saw a flame in the sky. Suspecting the explosion might have been the result of an accident at a nearby dynamite store, he broke off to investigate. He saw a large, shiny object standing on the ground and two figures dressed in white. He stopped to take a closer look, but the figures disappeared. Then he heard another roar, a blue flame sparked underneath the object, and it rose into the air. Zamora took cover and watched as the smooth, round vehicle sped across the desert at high speed. When a fellow officer arrived on the scene, he noted that Zamora was in shock, the dirt was disturbed and a bush was still burning.

HOLY SH!T

Several other witnesses reported seeing the egg-shaped object and its bluish flame, including a family whose car it had flown low over. Others heard the "roar" from a nearby town. Sand in the area had been turned into glass from extreme heat. An Air Force investigation failed to come to any conclusions, noting that Zamora was an unusually convincing witness.

FINAL SHIFT

In some hospitals patients are given different colour wristbands: white for new admissions, green for surgery, blue for discharged. The dead receive red wristbands on their way to the morgue.

An overworked junior doctor had finally reached the end of a double shift and called a lift to the ground floor. When the doors opened, it was empty except for a young woman in a hospital gown, heading for the basement.

On the next floor, an old man was waiting, and on seeing him the doctor leaped for the control panel and closed the doors.

"Didn't you see his wristband?" he asked the woman. "Only the dead wear red."

"Like this one?" she said.

THE GOOD SAMARITAN

Eighteen-year-old Robin Graham was driving home after a night out in November 1970. At 2 a.m. her Dodge ran out of gas on the Hollywood Freeway in California, USA. Passing police offered her a tow, but after she declined they directed her to a phone box so she could call for assistance. They later checked that Robin had made the call. The third time the police drove past, a blue Corvette had pulled up, and a man was peering under the Dodge's bonnet. Thinking it was a relative, the cops carried on. Robin's relatives turned up half an hour later. They found the Dodge, but Robin was nowhere to be found, and she was never seen again.

HOLY SH!T

Another woman was approached on the same road that night by a man claiming to be an off-duty policeman. He was driving a blue Corvette. The man was later identified as Bruce Davis, a convicted double murderer, a member of Charles Manson's gang and a suspect in the infamous Zodiac Killer case, currently serving a life sentence. Robin Graham's disappearance remains unsolved.

EYE-OPENING

In 2019 a woman in Taiwan was admitted to hospital after suffering extreme pain and tears in her right eye. A doctor was surprised to find what looked like insect legs in the affected eye. As he removed the objects with the help of a microscope, he realized with horror that they were bees, sweat bees, to be exact, and four of them, happily feeding on the tears produced by their painful presence.

HOLY SH!T

"Sweat bees" are common around the world and are attracted to human sweat and tears due to their salt content. On this occasion the bees had been blown into the patient's eye while she was tending a relative's grave. Fortunately the bees didn't sting her, and her eyesight was saved.

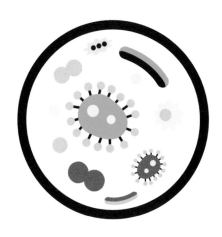

VIRAL CONSPIRACY

In 2013, an outbreak of Ebola virus killed more than 11,000 people in West Africa. It was the largest outbreak of the virus, which causes severe fever, deadly dehydration and internal bleeding, since it appeared in the Congo in 1976. On average only 50 per cent of those infected survive. That's bad enough, but some – including journalists, academics and a Liberian newspaper – claimed the pathogen was developed by the US government and released in Africa in secret trials, via vaccinations, supported by international health organizations. Motives include live tests for an antidote, population control and "bio-warfare" for control of West Africa.

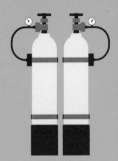

BREATHLESS

In 2012, Scottish deep-sea diver Chris Lemons was working with his colleague Dave on a pipeline almost 100 metres under the surface of the North Sea. Both were attached to a diving bell. When an alarm sounded they scrambled back to the bell – the ship was drifting, and Chris's air cable caught on the pipeline and snapped, leaving him in complete darkness at the bottom of the sea with about 5 minutes of backup oxygen. He soon blacked out. When Dave was finally able to retrieve him, Chris had been without oxygen for more than 30 minutes. But after receiving CPR, incredibly he started breathing again.

HOLY SH!T

Not only did Chris Lemons survive more than half an hour without oxygen, he suffered no lasting effects. How is a mystery. The near-freezing water may have helped, by slowing his body down, and Chris himself believes that the high concentration of oxygen in his backup supply allowed his body to store extra oxygen.

THE MULTIVERSE

What if Earth was not the only Earth? Or our universe was not the only universe? That's what scientists who came up with the multiverse theory of existence would have us believe. There are several different multiverse ideas (naturally) but the most mind-bending is the "many worlds" hypothesis. This theory, informed by quantum mechanics, says that the world is splitting into different realities at every moment, meaning that all the possible universes that can exist will exist at some point, but that an observer can only see one version. You could be both alive and dead, in two equally real universes, at the same time.

HOLY SH!T

The many worlds theory solves one of science's most famous thought experiments. "Schrödinger's cat" imagines that a theoretical cat in a box could be simultaneously alive and dead, and if you opened the box, either could be true. In the many worlds theory, the cat would be both dead and alive, in separate but equally real universes.

AMITYVILLE

In November 1974, 23-year-old Ronald DeFeo Jr murdered his family in their sleep at 112 Ocean Avenue, Amityville in Long Island, New York. A year later, another family moved in, but not for long. George Lutz began to wake up at 3.15 a.m. every morning – the time the murders took place. The family noticed strange odours and cold spots; swarms of flies; their daughter started seeing a pig-like creature with red eyes; green slime oozed from the doors; Kathy Lutz felt a sensation of being embraced by an unseen force; and George woke to see Kathy levitating from the bed, among other horrors. They left after 28 days.

HOLY SH!T

The Lutz family's time in the house was later made infamous in a book, and the film The Amityville Horror *(1979).*
Both George and Kathy passed a lie detector test when questioned about their experience.
As for the house, it passed through other families without incident and sold for $600,000 in 2017, although the address has been changed.

ANNABELLE

In the late 1960s in the US, a student nurse bought a Raggedy Anne doll at a junk shop. Soon after she found strange notes in her apartment and the doll started to appear in different rooms. A psychic found that the doll was possessed by a dead girl called Annabelle. When the doll's behaviour became "malicious and frightening" – a friend woke up with the doll staring at him and pressure around his throat – its owner sought the help of paranormal investigators Ed and Lorraine Warren, who believed that the doll was "inhabited by an inhuman spirit". They placed the doll in a locked glass case in their occult museum, where she sits to this day.

HOLY SH!T

Annabelle's story was first reported by the Warrens, and was the inspiration for the 2014 horror film Annabelle. *The doll seems to have retained her powers over the years: Lorraine Warren claims that a motorcyclist died in a crash shortly after being ejected from her museum for mocking Annabelle, ignoring her own warnings.*

LITTLE MORETON HALL

A crooked timber-framed Tudor manor house, Little Moreton Hall in Cheshire, England, has been described as being like something out of a fairy tale, but perhaps a nightmare might be more appropriate. Its sad history began when the Moreton family were forced to leave after the English Civil War, and the house fell into disrepair. A ghostly lady is said to walk the long gallery, where an occult hexagram can be seen, and the sobs and wails of a long-dead boy can be heard throughout the night in the old chapel. Pairs of ancient shoes have been found hidden in the walls, a failed attempt to ward off malevolent spirits.

HIGH-RISK SECURITY

In January 2019 an unidentified man was killed as he tried to access Area 51, or to give it its full title, the Nevada National Security Site. He failed to stop at a checkpoint at the top-secret desert base and was pursued for 8 miles, before getting out of his car and approaching officers with a mysterious "cylindrical object", at which point he was shot dead. No further details have been released by the authorities.

HOLY SH!T

In July 1947, there were rumours of at least one UFO crash-landing near Roswell, New Mexico. The wreckage and the bodies of its mysterious crew were allegedly spirited away by the US government to an Air Force base named Area 51 in Nevada. It is said that this is where alien technology is being "reverse-engineered" into top-secret military aircraft, and the alien pilots are in the deep freeze. Or so the story goes.

TERESA FIDALGO

In the mid-2000s a video surfaced online which the uploader claimed was found on the camera of a Portuguese filmmaker in 2003. The night-vision footage shows friends driving in the mountains before stopping to pick up a girl. She speaks only to say her name is Teresa and that she wants to go "there, ahead". Soon she points to the road, saying that was the place of her death. The camera pans to her suddenly disfigured, terrified face and the car crashes. Two died, but the girl was not traced until it was discovered that a Teresa Fidalgo had died in an accident in 1983 in the same location.

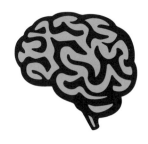

BRAIN IN A VAT

In *The Matrix* (1999) humans are kept alive in liquid-filled pods and fed a false reality controlled by machines. Some believe this is not so far-fetched. Our eyes can't "see" and our ears can't "hear" without our brain making their signals into what we experience as reality, so what's to say that the world even exists outside of our minds? We could all be disembodied brains in vats, being fed a false reality by a controlling force, and we would never know it.

HOLY SH!T

In 2018 it was revealed that scientists at Yale University had succeeded in keeping pig brains "alive" – that is, capable of normal activity – outside of the animals' bodies for several hours by supplying them with blood. Maybe the "brain in a vat" theory might be an actual possibility.

NETFLIX AND CHILLER

Late one night in July 2016, a boyfriend and girlfriend were watching Netflix at home in Chicago, USA, when they fell asleep on the couch. When they awoke, the woman's purse was missing, so they checked the security camera in the room for clues as to its whereabouts. What they saw chilled them to the bone. The footage showed a hooded intruder emerge from an upstairs bedroom and stand watching over the sleeping couple for at least 15 minutes. Then he disappeared. He was never traced.

THE RED ROOM

Japanese school children know all about the mysterious "Red Room" website. A window will appear suddenly when you're browsing the internet, seemingly at random. It is an animation on a red background, and a high-pitched voice will ask, "Do you like...?" If you close the window, it will pop up again. If you keep closing it, it will eventually ask, "Do you like the red room?" A long list of names will appear, with your own added at the bottom. It's said that every person on the list has disappeared...

HOLY SH!T

On 1 June 2004, an 11-year-old Japanese schoolgirl murdered a classmate with a pocket knife, slashing her wrists and throat. She blamed the crime on messages she had read on the internet. It emerged that the girl was obsessed with the "Red Room" website, leading to questions about its possible malign influence on Japanese youth.

THE PILOT

A boy who had just passed his test was driving through an old abandoned Air Force base in a remote part of East Anglia, England. His mind began to race with tales of ghostly pilots rumoured to appear in cars being driven across the old airfield. He knew it was nonsense, but he couldn't shake the feeling that he was not alone, so he stopped the car, turned all the interior lights on and looked around. Of course, there was nothing there. When he turned the lights off and looked back at the road, standing in his headlights was a man in a ragged flight suit, his head bent at a horrible angle, black eyes staring through the windscreen.

THE WATCHER

"Dearest new neighbour at 657 Boulevard. Allow me to welcome you to the neighbourhood".

It was June 2014 and the Broaddus family had yet to move into their newly purchased dream home in an exclusive neighbourhood in New Jersey, USA, when they received an odd letter. It started off friendly enough but then described the family's three children as *"young blood"* and asked, *"Do you know what lies within the walls? Why are you here? I will find out."* It was signed simply, "The Watcher". The family soon received more letters. *"Will the young blood play in the basement?... I would be very afraid if I were them... If you were upstairs you would never hear them scream,"* the Watcher threatened. They never moved in.

HOLY SH!T

The Watcher is still unidentified. The family went through a five-year nightmare trying to find the author of the letters, finally selling the house for a loss in 2019. Although the previous occupants of 657 Boulevard had recalled an odd letter that arrived days before they moved out, they received no other strange letters in the 20 years they had lived there.

THE DIARY OF IDILIA DUBBS

All I know is, my death is certain. Once more I will pray for the salvation of my soul, for you, father, mother, George and Marie. Then I will see whether I still have the strength to drag myself to the dark hope of the tower and to fall down. Oh, why did I not do it right away!

This was one of the final diary entries of Idilia Dubbs, a 17-year-old Scottish girl who went missing on holiday with her family in Germany in 1851. The pages were supposedly found near Idilia's skeleton in Lahneck Castle, Koblenz, nine years after she disappeared. The diary was reportedly kept under lock and key until it was published in 2010, with the proviso that "authenticity can never be entirely verified". The diaries record how Idilia became trapped at the top of the tower in the castle after a wooden staircase collapsed and depict her disintegrating mental state as she starved to death.

THE VAMPIRE OF DÜSSELDORF

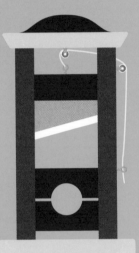

Tell me... after my head is chopped off, will I still be able to hear, at least for a moment, the sound of my own blood gushing from the stump of my neck? That would be the pleasure to end all pleasures.

These were the words of Peter Kürten as he was led to the guillotine. He committed at least nine murders around the German city of Düsseldorf in the 1910s and 1920s, and he attempted many more. His gruesome nickname referred to his fetish for blood, which he would drink from his victims.

HOLY SH!T

Kürten's severed head eventually found its way to the Ripley's Believe It or Not museum in Wisconsin, USA, where it can still be seen on display.

BACHELOR NO. 1

In 1978, Rodney Alcala appeared on TV in *The Dating Game* (a US version of *Blind Date*). He was charming and handsome, and he was picked ahead of two other bachelors by contestant Cheryl Bradshaw. Backstage, however, Bradshaw started to have regrets. "[Alcala] was acting really creepy… I didn't want to see him again." Her instincts probably saved her life. Alcala was a serial killer who had murdered at least three women in the year before his TV appearance, and he went on to kill at least three more afterward.

HOLY SH!T

Incredibly, Alcala was booked for the show despite a conviction for assaulting a young girl in 1972 and being on the FBI's list of Ten Most Wanted Fugitives. He was arrested in 1979, and has received several unfulfilled death sentences over the years.

GUIDED BY VOICES

A British woman presented to a London psychiatrist with an unusual complaint. She had heard strange voices in her head while sitting at home reading. "I know it must be shocking for you to hear me speaking to you like this," the voices said. "My friend and I used to work at Great Ormond Street hospital, and we would like to help you." The voices urged the woman to visit a hospital and request a brain scan. When the hospital reluctantly agreed to the scan, they discovered a brain tumour. After it was removed, the voices stopped.

JUST IMAGINE

The Beatles' John Lennon was murdered in New York on 8 December 1980. At 5 p.m. on that day a fan had snapped the last photos of the singer alive. In one picture Lennon can be seen signing a record for an autograph hunter. The man turned out to be Mark David Chapman, the man who would shoot and kill Lennon 6 hours later.

HOLY SH!T

Some believe that Chapman was brainwashed by the US government into killing Lennon. A secret (and genuine) CIA mind control programme known as Project MKUltra is usually blamed. The book The Catcher in the Rye, *which Chapman was carrying at the time, is thought to have been the "trigger" for Chapman to carry out the murder.*

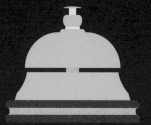

ROOM 333

Room 333 at the 150-year-old five-star Langham hotel – the highest numbered room in the hotel and still in use – is reportedly haunted by the ghost of a Victorian doctor who murdered his wife in the room and then committed suicide. Various people have reported disturbed nights in 333, including BBC journalists and England cricketers.

WHEN FALSE FLAGS ARE REAL

Operation Northwoods was a "false flag" operation proposed at the highest levels of the US Department of Defense in 1962. The plan was to commit false acts of terrorism in order to provoke a reaction against communist Cuba. Among the proposals to be blamed on Cuba were the blowing up of a US-registered ship, killing refugees, attacking a US Air Force jet and even shooting down a passenger plane. Fortunately, President Kennedy rejected the plan.

HOLY SH!T

To this day conspiracy theorists use the operation as evidence that Western governments are capable of false flag attacks, but Operation Northwoods wasn't quite as evil as it sounds. Elaborate ruses were designed to convince the public that real people had died in the attacks. For example, an empty remote-controlled plane would be passed off as a genuine passenger flight and shot down, while the real passengers were unloaded at a secret destination. However, the proposals did include the "wounding" of Cuban refugees and detonating genuine bombs.

LUCIA JOAQUIN

A story went viral in the Philippines that warned Facebook users about late-night messages from "Lucia Joaquin", who claimed to be a lonely young girl, but whose profile pic was too dark to make out. During the conversation Lucia asked if you could take a picture together. If you agreed, your phone camera or webcam flashed in your face. Then Lucia prompted you to ask her for a clearer photo of herself. The picture she sends is that one that your own phone just took, except there's a dark figure lurking in the background...

THE ENFIELD HAUNTING

Peggy Hodgson and her four children were having trouble sleeping. They were being kept awake by strange sounds of furniture moving throughout their home. A disturbed neighbour called police in August 1977, which brought a procession of journalists and paranormal investigators to the small house in Enfield, North London, England. At least thirty visitors reported witnessing unexplained phenomena such as chairs moving across rooms and knocking on walls; some even reported hearing a voice emanating from 11-year-old Janet Hodgson, and others claimed they had seen her levitate several feet into the air.

HOLY SH!T

Some blame the young sisters Janet and Margaret for faking all the events in the Enfield haunting, which is perhaps more disturbing than a genuine poltergeist haunting. The episode inspired The Conjuring *series of movies.*

THE BELL WITCH

The Bell Witch terrorized the Bell family of Adams, Tennessee, USA, in the early 1800s. It had the voice of a woman but could not be seen, and it would move objects and slap and pinch the Bell children. It was widely believed to be the spirit of Kate Batts, who felt cheated by a land deal with John Bell, the family patriarch, and swore that she would haunt the family. Many visitors to the house heard the witch, sometimes angry, sometimes singing. She would scream all night to keep the family awake and poke needles into their skin. When John Bell died in 1820, the Bell Witch was blamed; according to rumours she had replaced his regular medicine with poison.

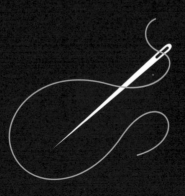

THE OMEN

On Friday 13 August 1976, special effects designer John Richardson, who had recently finished work on horror film *The Omen*, was in a car crash in which his passenger, Liz Moore, was decapitated. Months before Richardson had set up a famous decapitation scene for the movie, which was seemingly cursed from the beginning: actor Gregory Peck's plane was hit by lightning en route to England for filming; a flight chartered by the studio and swapped at the last minute crashed shortly after take-off; and an animal trainer was killed by a tiger days after working on the film.

HOLY SH!T

The Omen *producer Harvey Bernhard, who narrowly avoided a lightning strike while filming the movie in Rome, wore a cross on set and later said, "I really firmly believe that the devil didn't want us to make the film." On the way back from England to the USA, Bernhard's plane had to make an emergency landing. He was carrying the finished film with him.*

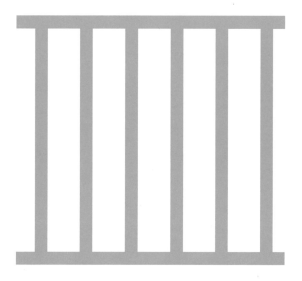

HUMAN ZOOS

The distinguished English scientist and inventor James Lovelock believes that cyborgs will rule the world within 100 years, as part of a natural process of evolution beyond humans. The cyborgs will probably not kill us all; he expects humans to be kept around like animals in a zoo. It's not all bad, though, as our new robotic overlords will use their super-intelligence and obedient human slaves to solve the climate crisis, cooling the planet and ensuring the survival of both species.

CALIFORNIA DREAMING

The Golden State Killer, a prolific murderer who took at least 13 lives and sexually assaulted more than 50 victims in the 1970s and 1980s, had a particularly creepy modus operandi. He would often stalk his victims for weeks, sometimes even knocking at their door and ringing them to figure out their routines. When he found an entry point, he would appear in their bedrooms wearing a ski mask, waking them with a flashlight or knocking on the door with his knife, calling their name. He would also ring his previous assault victims, sometimes years later, asking if they remembered his visit.

HOLY SH!T

The Golden State Killer taunted the police the day of several of his murders by calling up the police station and jeering at their incompetence. In April 2018 police apprehended Joseph DeAngelo, a 73-year-old former police officer, after DNA evidence linked him to the Golden State Killer case. He was charged with 13 murders and 13 kidnappings.

INTERDIMENSIONAL BEINGS

In 1997, an American satellite radio show hosted by Art Bell heard from an unidentified caller who claimed to work at Area 51. The highly agitated man, who stated that "they" would soon track his location, claimed that aliens are already here on Earth, but they are "extra-dimensional beings" that exist in a dimension humans can't detect. These aliens had allegedly infiltrated the US military establishment and were behind forthcoming disasters that would wipe out "major population centres". The satellite feed went down before he could say any more. The date of the call? September 11: four years to the day before the World Trade Center attacks in New York.

THE RUSSIAN APARTMENT BOMBINGS

In September 1999, five bombs exploded in four apartment buildings in cities around Russia. The government, including then-Prime Minister Vladimir Putin, quickly blamed Chechen terrorists. Many now believe that the Russian's own FSB (formerly the KGB) were behind the bombings. A military-grade explosive was used – something admitted then denied by the state. Most damningly, FSB agents were caught with explosives in another apartment that same month. They claimed it was a training exercise. After the bombings the Russians began a second war in Chechnya as "revenge", which paved the way for Vladimir Putin to become president.

HOLY SH!T

Prior to the attacks, at least one journalist predicted they would occur in Moscow to the benefit of ailing President Boris Yeltsin. Several people who voiced their misgivings have died in suspicious circumstances, including ex-FSB agent Alexander Litvinenko. His associate, billionaire Boris Berezovsky, part of Yeltsin's inner circle at the time of the attacks, repeatedly said the FSB was behind them. He was the subject of several alleged assassination plots while living in Britain and was found hanged in 2013.

THE FINAL PATIENT

Jenny was waiting alone in a hospital clinic. It was getting late, and most of the staff had gone home. Footsteps echoed down a corridor, and a small old woman wearing a patient's gown and dragging an IV drip shuffled into view. She sat down across from 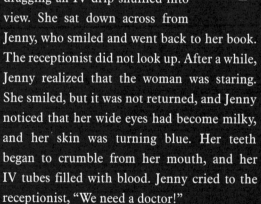 Jenny, who smiled and went back to her book. The receptionist did not look up. After a while, Jenny realized that the woman was staring. She smiled, but it was not returned, and Jenny noticed that her wide eyes had become milky, and her skin was turning blue. Her teeth began to crumble from her mouth, and her IV tubes filled with blood. Jenny cried to the receptionist, "We need a doctor!"

"For who?" came the reply. "You're the only one here. And the doctor will see you now."

THE RAPTURE

It's estimated that 15 million American Christians believe in "the rapture", an apocalyptic prophecy that promises that sometime soon Jesus will return to Jerusalem and all true believers will ascend into heaven along with the resurrected spirits of dead Christians. The world will be destroyed in the Battle of the Armageddon and survivors will convert or go to hell. Part of the belief is that the Jewish people must gather in Jerusalem, where the war will begin, so the creation of Israel in 1948 proves that the rapture is on its way.

HOLY SH!T

When President Trump declared in 2017 that the capital of Israel was Jerusalem, and moved the US embassy to the city, evangelicals took it as another sign that he was on their side, and that the rapture was proceeding as planned.

THE SALT AND PEPPER LADY

In the town of Devine, Texas, USA, residents are encouraged to ignore knocking at their doors in the early hours. If they listen at the door, they might hear an old woman asking for salt and pepper. The few people who have opened the door have reported seeing a decomposed body with no eyes, the wrists slit, and horribly swollen with water. It's said that the "salt and pepper lady" killed herself in the bath, and in the afterlife remains angry at the neighbours who ignored her while she was alive.

WAR PLAN RED

In the late 1930s the United States devised secret plans for an invasion of Canada, as part of a war with Britain. "War Plan Red" identified that Britain would use Canada as a springboard to invade the US, so pre-emptive strikes against Canadian targets would be required as a defensive measure. Having repelled an invasion, the United States would win the war eventually by starving Britain with a naval blockade. It sounds like a conspiracy theory, but it's all true.

HOLY SH!T

War Plan Red-Orange was a similar scheme, but imagined the strategy required if the United States faced war on two fronts, with the UK and Japan simultaneously.

LESS THAN HUMAN

Of the trillions of cells that make up your body, more than 50 per cent are not human at all. No matter how much you shower, the human body plays host to vast quantities of bacteria, fungi and viruses that thrive in every nook and cranny, but particularly in the gut. It sounds disgusting, but what scientists call your "microbiome" is vital for your health. It seems that the microbiome means that genes tell only half the story of what it means to be human.

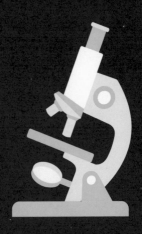

SIMMERING THREAT

One of the world's largest active supervolcanoes sits under Yellowstone National Park, one of America's most popular destinations. The Yellowstone Caldera is thought to "super erupt" every 700,000 years; the last one happened 650,000 years ago. Under the volcano's 45-mile-wide crater sits a 5-mile-deep pool of hot magma. A super eruption would kill thousands, spew volcanic ash for thousands of miles, a metre deep in places, decimating crops and affecting the global climate.

HOLY SH!T

Super eruptions are thought to occur somewhere in the world every 100,000 years. The Toba eruption in Indonesia 76,000 years ago is said to have caused a ten-year winter and nearly wiped out early humanity.

A LIGHT ON THE PAST

The Andromeda Galaxy is widely regarded as the farthest object visible with the naked eye. When we view the cluster of stars we are looking back in time more than 2.5 million years, when its light started the long journey to Earth. What you see now is what the galaxy looked like when some of *Homo sapiens'* earliest "human" ancestors were alive, and sabre-toothed tigers roamed the Americas. In that period of time, Andromeda could have disappeared; but it would take 2.5 million years for us to notice.

POLYBIUS

The video game arcades of 1980s Portland, Oregon, USA, were abuzz with excitement about a new machine that had appeared in town. Polybius was so popular that kids would queue around the block. They became obsessed to the point of fighting over the controls and began to suffer dizziness, memory loss, nightmares and suicidal tendencies. It's said that mysterious men in black suits turned up periodically to examine the machines, and then, as quickly as the game had appeared, Polybius disappeared. The rumours are that it was a secret government mass-psychology experiment of unknown purpose.

THE LOST COSMONAUTS

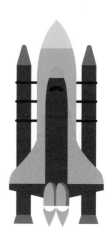

A persistent conspiracy theory alleges that several Russian cosmonauts were launched into space before Yuri Gagarin's 1961 mission, when he became the first man in space. We don't know about them because it is supposed that their deaths were covered up by Soviet authorities. The theory draws on several sources, including disturbing recordings made in the 1960s by the Judica-Cordiglia brothers, amateur astronomers from Turin, Italy, who claimed to have intercepted the communications of space missions. In 1960 they recorded an SOS signal in Morse code from a spacecraft thought to be drifting away from Earth's orbit into space. Their tapes also supposedly capture the last moments of several unidentified cosmonauts as they were launched to their various deaths, suffocating as their air ran out, burning to death in the Earth's atmosphere or drifting helplessly out of control.

THE YELLOW BEETLE

Drivers on the Karak highway in Malaysia are warned to watch out for a battered yellow VW Beetle that approaches at great speed from behind, overtakes and then forces drivers to stop. It is rumoured that there is nobody in the driver's seat and if you overtake, you will encounter bad luck down the road, likely an accident, and possibly death.

CLOSE CALL

On the night of 22 March 1970, Kathleen Johns was driving with her baby daughter on a California highway when the car behind started flashing its headlights. When she pulled over the driver said her rear wheel was loose and offered to fix it. Kathleen agreed, but when she pulled away, the wheel fell off. She accepted the man's offer of a lift, but he refused to stop, driving around for hours, until Kathleen managed to escape with her daughter at a junction and hide in a field until he left. Later, at a police station, she noticed the man on a poster; he was wanted for murder.

HOLY SH!T

Four months later the San Francisco Chronicle *received a letter referring to the "woman and her baby that I gave a rather interesting ride for a couple of hours one evening a few months back". It was from "The Zodiac", an unidentified serial killer who murdered at least five people.*

"SUSIE'S DYING"

British people of a certain age might remember the 1970s activity of calling up a certain number – often recalled as consisting of zeros, ones and twos – in a phone box and hearing a voice on the other end repeatedly intone, "Help! Help me! Susie's dying." Nobody knows who Susie was or who was on the other end of the line, and it's unlikely that we'll ever find out.

UNIDENTIFIED FRIGHTENING OBJECT

In 2014 two US Air Force F/A-18 fighter jets flying from the USS *Theodore Roosevelt* aircraft carrier were reported to have had a near-miss with another craft off the coast of Virginia. The shocked pilots reported that a sphere had flown right between the planes, which were only 100 feet apart. Fellow pilots had reported seeing objects on their radar systems, but this was the first visual contact. The mysterious craft had no obvious propulsion but hit speeds estimated at 4,000 miles per hour and made sudden turns that would have killed any human crew onboard. The sightings continued for months but stopped when the aircraft carrier left US waters.

HOLY SH!T

In 2019 members of the United States Senate received a classified briefing from the US Navy after an increase in UFO sightings. The same year, the Pentagon announced a new UFO reporting system for incidents such as those experienced by the crew of the USS Theodore Roosevelt, *or, as they put it, "a series of intrusions by advanced aircraft on Navy carrier strike groups".*

INNER SPACE

It may surprise you to learn that 99.9999 per cent of your body is empty space. The mass of each atom that makes up humans is almost entirely contained in the nucleus, which is surrounded by electrons orbiting in, well, nothing. If you could remove the empty space – which would be extremely hard, not to mention painful – the whole human population could be compressed into a volume no bigger than a tennis ball.

BOHEMIAN GROVE

Each year, a who's who of America's most powerful men gather at a private compound north of San Francisco to network, lay on bawdy entertainment and take part in a secret ritual for which they are sworn to secrecy.

The annual gathering at Bohemian Grove for members of the Bohemian Club of San Francisco has been taking place since the nineteenth century. Members have included US presidents Teddy Roosevelt, Richard Nixon, Ronald Reagan and George H. W. Bush, alongside powerful industrialists, media magnates and celebrities. The event is notoriously secretive, and the central "Cremation of Care" ritual – in which hooded figures burn an effigy on an altar in front of a giant owl statue – had never been made public until conspiracy theorist Alex Jones gained entrance in 2000 and captured it on film. The meaning of the ceremony is not entirely clear; according to conspiracy theorists, it's devil worship. To them, Bohemian Grove is where men who rule the world pick presidents, plan wars and bond over satanic rites rumoured to include actual human sacrifice.

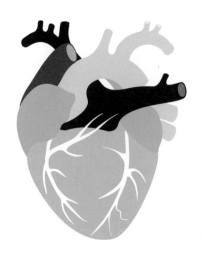

ORGAN DONATION

During the 1998–99 conflict in Kosovo, the Kosovo Liberation Army (KLA) took many Serbs captive. After the war, it's said that the KLA took them across the border into Albania, where their organs were harvested for sale on the black market, an assertion that a 2014 EU report found "compelling indications" to support. One witness claimed that he was "trained" by a doctor on how to remove organs, and that he removed the heart from a man who was still alive – and awake – with a bayonet. The heart was then taken to the local airport and flown out of the country.

THE ILLUMINATI

It is rumoured to be a secret yet all-powerful group that manipulates global events as part of a grand plot to establish a global government – the so-called "New World Order". Conspiracy theorists allege that this powerful secret society is the hidden hand behind much of modern history. The group is rumoured to include billionaires, international politicians, captains of industry, the aristocracy and even members of the British royal family. According to the theories, those working toward the New World Order plan to recreate a world of rulers and the ruled, with a single global currency and no borders.

HOLY SH!T

The Illuminati are claimed to be so powerful that they were behind both World Wars (and all others since), the assassinations of President Kennedy, Martin Luther King and John Lennon, the 2008 financial crisis and even natural disasters such as the 2001 Boxing Day tsunami. They are thought to manipulate the masses using mind-control techniques such as subliminal messages in television shows and music videos.

THE CLINTON BODY COUNT

The "Clinton body count", a list that has been circulating online for years, claims that Bill and Hillary Clinton have left a number of "suspicious" deaths in their wake since Bill's reign as Governor of Arkansas, most notably Vincent Foster, a Clinton aide who committed suicide in 1993. The list also includes several army officers and guards who provided security for the Clintons, and Secretary of Commerce Ronald H. Brown, who died in a helicopter crash. The body count was updated in 2019 by right-wing activists to account for the deaths of ex-politicians from Arkansas and New York police officers, and even Hillary's own brother.

THE SETH RICH CONSPIRACY

On 10 July 2016, 27-year-old Seth Rich, a staffer at the Democratic National Committee, was walking home in Washington, D.C., USA, when he was accosted by two men. He resisted and was shot and killed in what police suspected to be a botched robbery. Internet reports began to question the story – why did robbers leave Rich's wallet? A story emerged that Rich was killed because of his alleged involvement in the infamous leak of internal Democratic party emails to Wikileaks. His killers have not been found.

HOLY SH!T

In 2019 it emerged that the idea that Rich was murdered as part of a political conspiracy was first seeded online by Russian intelligence services. The bulletin was part of a concerted disinformation drive to disrupt the 2016 presidential campaign. It first appeared just three days after Rich's death.

KNOCK, KNOCK, KNOCK

Try this next time you're in a Japanese school and you're feeling brave: find a bathroom on the third floor and knock three times on the door of the third cubicle. Ask, "Are you there, Hanako-san?" Then wait. If you hear a girl reply, it's said to be the voice of a young schoolgirl who committed suicide in the bathroom long ago. Allegedly, the door will open, and if you're lucky you will find the cubicle empty. But you might see the bloodied ghost of Hanako-san crouching on the floor, waiting. Before you can react she'll drag you into the toilet and drown you.

SLEEPER CELL

In July 2019, as the diplomatic situation between the UK and Iran heated up over the seizure of a British-flagged oil tanker, newspapers revealed UK intelligence agency fears that Iranian-funded sleeper cells were already in place in the UK and Europe, and would receive the green light for terrorist attacks if the two countries went to war. The cells were thought to be linked to Hezbollah, a Lebanese militant group supported by Iran.

HOLY SH!T

In 2015 police discovered that a Hezbollah-linked sleeper cell was stockpiling tonnes of ammonium nitrate in ice packs in London – the same explosive material that was used in the 1995 Oklahoma City bombing. The raid was only revealed in 2019.

JUST A CHECK-UP

In 2014, an Indonesian woman had just arrived in Qatar to start a new job. Her employer requested that she have a medical before she start work. At the hospital a doctor gave her an injection against her will, and she lost consciousness. When she awoke, she was in excruciating pain and had an incision scar on her stomach. She was given no explanation for the incident and life carried on as normal... except for the fact that she repeatedly fell ill, and soon had to return home to Indonesia. Several years later, after suffering severe pain in her side, she sought medical help. An X-ray revealed that she was missing a kidney.

THE NUMBER OF THE BEAST

The rise of the "cashless society" has sparked fears among some Christians of a plot by world leaders and bankers to increase control and surveillance over members of the public. They believe that the end of cash signals the arrival of the "number of the beast" prophesied in the Book of Revelation: "He [the antichrist] causes all... to receive a mark on their right hand or on their foreheads, and that no one may buy or sell except one who has the mark or the name of the beast." The modern equivalent will be a barcode tattoo or a microchip implant.

HOLY SH!T

Many people in tech and body modification communities have voluntarily had microchips implanted under their skin. With the rise of contactless payments, it's not much of a stretch to imagine humans paying for their shopping with their skin.

103

INSIDE JOB?

When the twin towers collapsed in New York on 9/11, they took down several nearby buildings with them, but 7 World Trade Center remained standing for several hours. Then firefighters were ordered to pull back from the tower, and it collapsed like the others. Was it a controlled demolition? It wasn't hit by a plane and it doesn't look seriously damaged in the footage. Suspicions about 7WTC have led some to question the entire narrative of the 9/11 attacks; maybe the planes didn't bring the towers down on their own; maybe al-Qaeda weren't behind it at all?

NIBIRU

According to a translation of an ancient Sumerian cuneiform tablet, there is a secret planet called Nibiru, or Planet X, that orbits Earth every 3,600 years. Conspiracy theorists, initially led by a psychic who claimed to have been informed of the danger by distant aliens, believe that Nibiru is due to return sometime in the near future, and it will come dangerously close to our planet. Many claim that a "near-miss" flyby of hundreds of thousands of miles will be enough to swap the Earth's magnetic poles, sending the weather system haywire and wiping out humanity. They even believe it's already influencing natural disasters and is being kept a secret by NASA.

HOLY SH!T

Many believed that Planet X was due to collide with Earth in 2012, coinciding with the end of the calendar of the lost Mayan civilization. The planet never materialized (or you wouldn't be reading this).

THE CREDIT
CARD UNIVERSE

In 2017 a multinational team of astrophysicists observed irregularities in space that could change the way you look at the world. The evidence supports the theory that the entire universe is a hologram. Yes, that would mean you are experiencing the world in the same way Princess Leia appears to Obi-Wan Kenobi in *Star Wars*. The theory states that reality is a 3D illusion generated by a flat (yet balloon-shaped) 2D universe, which projects information – i.e. our entire reality – into the centre. Think about that next time you see a 3D movie. But not too hard.

OOPS!

In 1968 a United States Air Force B-52 bomber carrying four nuclear devices crashed near Thule Air Base in Greenland. Three of the bombs exploded, but a nuclear explosion was avoided. Nonetheless highly radioactive material was blasted over the area. The fourth bomb is thought to be lying dormant under the ice, and it's possible that the warhead could still function today.

HOLY SH!T

In 1961 two 4-megaton nuclear weapons were actually dropped on North Carolina after a B-52 bomber broke up following a mid-air refuelling mishap. Each bomb was 250 times more powerful than the 1945 Hiroshima explosion, but thankfully they did not detonate.

RED ROOMS

Hidden in the mysterious "dark web", a network of websites beyond the reach of Google, are black markets for drugs, guns and hacked data. More disturbing are the infamous "red rooms", which are rumoured to be exclusive platforms where users pay large amounts in untraceable cryptocurrency in order to watch live streams of torture and even murder. It's said that users who pay top dollar can control the crimes themselves. The existence of red rooms has never been confirmed.

ARE WE ALONE IN THE UNIVERSE?

The Fermi Paradox asserts that it's highly likely that intelligent life exists on other planets, but if it does, they should have visited Earth by now. The theory, named after Italian-American physicist Enrico Fermi, assumes that as there are billions of stars in the universe just like our Sun, there's a high probability that some will be orbited by Earth-like planets: therefore extraterrestrial life is likely to have evolved at some point in the past few billion years. Yet if these life forms developed interstellar travel, as we are likely to, where are their spaceships? Maybe we are alone after all.

HOLY SH!T

One answer to the Fermi Paradox is the idea that all intelligent life is destined to wipe itself out with its own technology – nuclear weapons for example. Intelligent aliens may have evolved, visited Earth, then died out millions of years before life here even got started.

PHOTOBOMB

In the fifteenth century a gamekeeper living in woodland near Grimsby, UK, left to fight in the Wars of the Roses. When he didn't return, his young wife took to wandering the woods with their baby son, where she eventually died of grief. Almost 600 years later two schoolgirls were taking selfies in the wood when they spotted something in one of their photos. A dark figure stood in the background. It appeared to be carrying something in its arms. They swiped to the next image and gasped – there was an extra face in the photo, pale grey, open-mouthed and contorted in grief.

HEAD CASE

An American woman who had recently returned from a trip to South America visited doctors after being ill for weeks and suffering violent seizures. A brain scan revealed a growth, which doctors investigated in a 6-hour operation, during which the patient remained awake because of the sensitive area being probed. The surgeons were shocked to discover that the growth was caused by a tapeworm that had burrowed deep into her brain. The parasite, carried by some infected meat the woman had eaten, had hatched in her guts before travelling through her bloodstream to the skull.

THE GREY GOO SCENARIO

Nanotechnology is a science that aims to build machines that are so small that they can manipulate molecules, or even atoms. The possibilities are endless, as a nanomachine could theoretically build anything it liked as long as the right molecules were in the right order. Even better, they would self-replicate. But that's where the problems might start. Left to their own (nano) devices, the tiny machines could theoretically deconstruct everything on Earth at a molecular level, converting the material into yet more versions of themselves, until there would be nothing left but the nanobots; something scientists have termed the "grey goo" scenario.

JUST FOLLOWING ORDERS

In the 1960s, psychologist Stanley Milgram conducted experiments in which normal people were encouraged to inflict increasingly powerful electric shocks on another person when ordered to, as part of what they were told was a "learning" experiment. The shocks were fake, but they seemed real. The highest voltages were labelled "danger: severe shock", then simply "XXX", suggesting death. The victim, or "learner", was in a different room, and pre-recorded screams and banging sounds were played as the "shocks" were triggered. Participants could end the experiment if they wanted, but incredibly more than 60 per cent went on to administer the maximum lethal voltage.

HOLY SH!T

In one experiment, the test subject was informed that the learner had a heart condition, but that didn't stop the electric shocks. Milgram's experiments were inspired by Nazi war crimes: how far will normal people go to inflict cruelty under orders from an authority figure? Similar experiments have largely confirmed his findings. In a recent Polish study, 90 per cent of the participants inflicted the highest voltages.

THE EXORCISM OF ANNELIESE MICHEL

Anneliese Michel of Leipzig, Germany, started suffering from epilepsy and psychosis at a young age. When highly religious Anneliese started to experience demonic hallucinations, hearing voices saying she would rot in hell, and became sensitive to crucifixes, her family sought an exorcism. The priests claimed she was possessed by Hitler, Judas Iscariot and Emperor Nero, that she would roar *"sieg heil"* and smash her head against the floor. She suffered injuries to her knees from constant praying. Anneliese underwent 60 exorcisms, but she only worsened, eventually refusing food and doctors. The 23-year-old died of starvation in July 1976, weighing just 30 kg.

HOLY SH!T

Anneliese's parents and two Catholic priests were put on trial for negligent homicide. They were given a suspended sentence, as it was thought the family had suffered enough. The judge found that Anneliese's life could have been saved as late as ten days before her death had they sought medical treatment.

THE GIANT TIC TAC

A US Navy pilot was flying over the Pacific Ocean when he was asked to check out a strange flying object detected on radar. When he arrived at the location, he saw what he could only describe as a giant "Tic Tac", 40 feet long, with no wings, windows or engines. The object dropped from 30,000 feet to sea level in less than a second – an impossible manoeuvre – and turned the calm sea to froth. When he flew closer, the vessel disappeared so quickly that he could not give chase, and the encounter remains a mystery.

AN AFTERLIFE SENTENCE

A locksmith was working in an abandoned jail in Philadelphia, USA, where he often felt that he was being watched. He opened a cell and was suddenly paralysed by an unseen force. Anguished faces of tortured souls appeared on the cell walls, and one beckoned him inside. The prison was Eastern State Penitentiary, first opened in 1829 as supposedly a more humane jail, but today the past suffering of inmates haunts the building, renowned as one of the most haunted places in America. Visitors report hearing tortured screams, sadistic laughter, cell doors slamming and an angry presence hiding in the dark.

HOLY SH!T

Eastern State was "less violent" than other jails but more disturbing. Inmates were locked up for 23 hours a day without sunlight, forbidden from talking and always hooded outside their cells. Punishments included being strapped to a chair so tightly that limbs were amputated and being made to wear an iron gag that tore the tongue out. The worst offenders were locked in cramped concrete tombs dug underground, where they would stew for weeks.

THE CRYING BOY

In 1985, a fire burned down a house in Rotherham, England. When firefighters picked through the ashes, they found a portrait of a crying boy, completely unscathed. It was later revealed that the fire service had found copies of the same portrait in the aftermath of several house fires, and it was always untouched by the flames. A few months after the first inferno, a house in Surrey was similarly wrecked, just six months after the crying boy was hung on its walls. The crying boy is rumoured to be a street urchin who witnessed his parents' fiery death in World War Two.

ACOUSTIC ATTACK

Between 2016 and 2018, dozens of diplomatic staff who worked in the US embassy in Cuba reported falling ill with headaches, dizziness, insomnia and balance problems after hearing penetrating grinding or chirping noises in their homes, or the sound of air buffeting through a car window. Suspecting that they had been attacked with some kind of sonic weapon, the US government withdrew half of the staff in Havana. Scans on 40 of the victims reportedly showed unexpected and unexplained abnormalities in brain tissue, and the sound was never identified.

HOLY SH!T

Acoustic weapons are not the stuff of science fiction. Low frequency "sound cannons", used to repel pirates and control protesters, are so powerful that targets have been known to literally sh*t themselves. This was not the experience of the American diplomats, however. Some experts believe the sound the US embassy staff heard was not a sonic weapon but caused by accidental ultrasonic noises, possibly produced by surveillance equipment. Others claim that the offending sound was the mating call of the Indies short-tailed cricket.

STULL CEMETERY

Stull Cemetery in Kansas, USA, is reputed to host a genuine gateway to hell, said to be stone steps in an unknown location that lead deep underground. The devil allegedly makes an appearance twice a year, on Halloween and the spring equinox, and a grave in the cemetery is rumoured to hold the remains of the devil's own child. A tree which grows out of the grave is thought to be a hanging tree where witches were executed, and the cemetery's torn-down church was a centre for black magic.

THE SINGULARITY

The Singularity is a proposed point in the near future when artificial intelligence learns to evolve on its own and computers will become smarter than the humans who created them. Once this happens, computers with an intelligence beyond human understanding will rapidly take over the world. Such super-intelligent machines, free of human programming, may decide that we are simply no longer necessary...

HOLY SH!T

The threat of artificial intelligence has been taken seriously by some big names in science and technology:

"At least when there's an evil dictator, that human is going to die. But for an [artificial intelligence], there would be no death. It would live forever. And then you'd have an immortal dictator from which we can never escape." – Elon Musk, 2018

"The development of full artificial intelligence could spell the end of the human race." – Stephen Hawking, 2014

THE ANNUNAKI

The most powerful people in the world are not even human beings, according to a theory most associated with former BBC sports reporter David Icke. Our leaders are in fact vampiric shape-shifting alien lizards, bred with humans to create humanoid hybrids. Their aim is to enslave mankind and they are responsible for atrocities throughout history, from the Holocaust to 9/11. Anyone wielding power could be a secret reptile, from celebrities to world leaders to the British royal family. The "Annunaki", or "Archons", arrived in ancient times, appeared as gods to early civilizations and are said to be the "Nephilim" referred to in the Bible.

HOLY SH!T

David Icke has more than 600,000 followers and tens of millions of views on his YouTube channel for his conspiracy theories, has published popular books and performs to sold-out arenas.

TRINITY

On 16 July 1945, the first atomic bomb explosion took place in the New Mexico desert in the USA, a test codenamed Trinity. The risks of detonating the biggest man-made explosion in history were not taken lightly by the team of physicists at Los Alamos laboratories. In 1942, fears were raised that the bomb could set off a chain reaction that would ignite Earth's atmosphere, burning the sky and ending all life on Earth. It was taken seriously, but scientists calculated that it was a three in 10 billion chance, which was deemed an acceptable risk. But still, it wasn't *impossible*.

HOLY SH!T

The Trinity explosion was likened to a "dirty bomb", as it showered thousands of square miles with radioactive material. Evidence collected by the New Mexico authorities shows an unusually high infant mortality rate in areas downwind from the test site, particularly in the months afterward.

THE GUNDIAH INCIDENT

Amy Rylance was asleep in the lounge of the mobile home she shared with her husband in Gundiah, Australia, while her friend Petra slept in another room. At 11.15 p.m. Petra woke to find Amy floating out of an open window, still asleep, carried by a beam of light toward what she described as a "flying saucer". The police were called, and while still on the scene they received word that a woman matching Amy's description had walked into a gas station in the bush near Mackay, dehydrated and unsure of her identity. But Mackay is almost 500 miles from Gundiah. The case remains a mystery.

A VERY PERSONAL HAUNTING

Esther Cox, a 19-year-old from Nova Scotia, Canada, was hearing strange noises under her bed. One night her body began to swell and her skin became scalding hot to the touch. Her family watched helplessly as she screamed in pain. There was a deafening bang from under the bed and her condition suddenly eased, but not for long. Invisible slaps would leave red marks on Esther's face, something jabbed pins in her limbs and unexplained fires would start in the house. A doctor witnessed Esther's bedclothes moving of their own accord as she slept and saw the words "ESTHER COX YOU ARE MINE TO KILL" scrawled in the ceiling plaster.

HOLY SH!T

When Esther sought refuge from the spirit in a church, the service was disrupted after an invisible force began banging on the walls. Esther's manifestations ended in November 1879, following a four-month jail sentence for allegedly burning down a friend's barn.

PIZZAGATE

In December 2016 a man armed with a rifle entered Comet Pizza in Washington, D.C., USA, and fired three times as part of what he called an "investigation" into child sex slaves, who he thought were being kept prisoner in tunnels under the restaurant. But he wasn't just a lone crazy; many people believed that the location was connected to a powerful paedophile ring with links to the Democratic Party, which is now known as the "Pizzagate" conspiracy.

HOLY SH!T

Pizzagate sprouted in the dark far-right corners of the internet, after Democratic Party emails were leaked during the 2016 presidential election campaign. Some believed that the leaked emails contained code words for a sex-trafficking conspiracy that used tunnels underneath Washington, D.C. businesses.

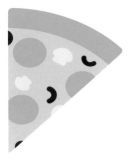

IN THE FLESH

Before Debbie Harry became a star with Blondie, she had another brush with fame. Late one night in 1972 she accepted a lift from a man driving a Volkswagen Beetle in Manhattan. When she saw that the car had no handles for the doors or windows, Harry panicked but managed to stretch her hand out of a gap in the window, open the moving car door and tumble out onto the road. Seventeen years later, Harry saw the man's face on the news. It was Ted Bundy, America's most notorious serial killer, and he was known to drive a modified Beetle. He had just been executed.

IMAGE CREDITS

If you're interested in finding out more about our books, find us on Facebook at **Summersdale Publishers** and follow us on Twitter at **@Summersdale**.

www.summersdale.com